Back Harbour

Front Harbour

OLD TOWN

LUNENBURG

Map source: Council of Maritime Premiers, Land Registration and Information service (LRIS), topographic series based on 1981 aerial photography.

BUILDINGS OF
OLD LUNENBURG

Terry James & Bill Plaskett

NIMBUS
PUBLISHING

To our children,
Rachel James
Anna & Joel Plaskett

Nimbus Publishing Limited
PO Box 9301, Station A
Halifax, NS B3K 5N5
902 (455-4286)

Design: Semaphor Design Co. Inc., Halifax
Printed and bound in Hong Kong by Everbest Printing Co. Ltd.

Nimbus Publishing acknowledges the support of the Canadian Council and the Department of Canadian Heritage.

Canadian Cataloguing in Publication Data
James, Terry.
Buildings of old Lunenburg
ISBN 1-55109-153-4
1. Lunenburg (N.S.)—Buildings, structures, etc. 2. Architecture—Nova Scotia—Lunenburg. I. Plaskett, Bill. II. Title.
FC2349.L85Z57 1996   720'.9716'23   C95-950318-8
F1039.5L86J35 1996

PREFACE

IT WAS FIFTEEN YEARS AGO that I first wandered the streets of old Lunenburg. From my experience of other Maritime towns, I could almost intuit that there would be a broad King Street running from a town square down to the harbour. I was unprepared, though, for the crowding of so many wood-framed buildings close to sidewalks and to each other; for the variation of shapes and styles; for the distinctive "Bumps" and brackets. A genuine quality to the place remains intact, apparent not only in the grit of waterfront industry and in the still incongruous encroachments of modern commerce, but more importantly from a sense that this place has been around for a long time. Indeed, by North American standards Lunenburg is old—two-and-one-half centuries old. Spared the ravages of fires, Lunenburg is that rare expression of an enterprising people who have shaped and reshaped with wood the spirit of their own place.

As a photographer, in my negotiations with narrow streets, summer traffic, the shadows of trees, and the position of the sun, I have aimed to let the buildings speak for themselves. Working with a wood-field camera of venerable design, I sought to record the essential forms. Many structures readily revealed themselves; others proved recalcitrant.

On questions of selection, a number of factors were at play and not all were deliberate. As for peeling paint, cluttered windowsills, and other signs of life, they were recorded with intent. Lunenburg is an honest town, and I would not want to belie the integrity of its character.

I am indebted to Bill Plaskett for a concise introduction and insightful captions to the photographs. The depth of Bill's understanding of the story of Lunenburg's architecture and his efforts on behalf of Nova Scotian architectural preservation are well known. I enjoyed our collaborative effort.

Beatrice Renton, Lunenburg's Town Manager, has been very helpful with this project. Many other residents of Lunenburg have offered assistance and friendship. I also wish to thank, in Halifax, Steven Slipp at Semaphor Design and Dorothy Blythe, Dan Soucoup, and Joanne Elliott at Nimbus Publishing for their contributions towards this book.

Terry James

WHEN I FIRST SET FOOT in Lunenburg in 1975, the town was in the beginning stages of its transformation from a slightly run-down fishing port into the flagship of tourism in Nova Scotia. The Fisheries Museum had been in operation for a few years, but had yet to be federally assisted and renamed the "Fisheries Museum of the Atlantic." The railway tracks still ran along the waterfront as far as the Government Wharf, although trains were few. The commercial section of Lincoln Street was a pothole zone seriously in need of fixing. The Lunenburg Heritage Society was newly formed and enthusiastically embarking upon its first architectural restoration project. The excitement of the first craft festival was in the air.

In the twenty years since then, all of these indicators of change have moved several notches along the scale of progress. The museum parking lot is now fully paved to accommodate the annual summer flood of tour buses and motor homes. Lincoln Street, too, is now smooth sailing. The railway tracks were removed in the late 1980s, and Water Street—the rough, service road that once ran beside the tracks—has been rebuilt and renamed Bluenose Drive. Many old houses and industrial buildings within sight of the harbour have been turned into guest homes, restaurants or gift shops, and many other old houses have been painstakingly restored by new owners who have realized their historical value. At the same time, about twenty per cent of the town's old wooden houses are now covered in vinyl siding, and property values have risen three- and four-fold.

As a conservation planner, I am fascinated by these types of changes and the burgeoning tension between the need to keep things the same, for the purposes of heritage conservation and tourism promotion, and the need to preserve the spirit of "progress and enterprise" (and therefore change) that has always been at the heart of the town's economy.

For my part, I am very pleased to have worked with Terry James on this book. It has been a pleasure to revisit Lunenburg through his "photographer's eye" and to follow him through his interesting choices of image and his keen sense of form and detail. In writing the introduction, I have attempted to outline the most significant elements of the town's history while focusing on the main theme of architecture. Of necessity, much has had to be left out. For those readers interested in more detail, Mather B. DesBrisay's *History of Lunenburg County* is invaluable, as are Winthrop Bell's *History of the Foreign Protestants* and H.R. Balcom's *History of the Lunenburg Fishery.* In writing the captions, I have attempted to be brief as possible, in order to let the photographs speak for themselves, except in those cases where matters of historical or architectural interest warrant more detailed exposition. More detailed information on a building-by-building basis is available in *An Inventory of Lunenburg's Historic Buildings.*

Bill Plaskett

LUNENBURG OLD TOWN AND FRONT HARBOUR VIEWED FROM THE EAST.

The towers of the Lunenburg Academy and spire of Zion Lutheran Church can be seen on top of the hill. The schooner approaching the wharf on the left is the Bluenose II, *beyond which are the masts of HMS* Bounty, *the saltbanker* Theresa E. Connor *and the barquentine* Concordia. *Fishing company wharves line the waterfront.*

HMS BOUNTY AT THE SHIPYARDS

This replica of HMS Bounty *was built at the Smith & Rhuland shipyard in 1960 for the MGM movie "Mutiny on the Bounty." In 1995, the vessel paid a return visit to Lunenburg and is seen here moored near the boatshop where construction took place. This is the same shipyard where the* Bluenose *and the* Bluenose II *were built. Richard Smith and George Rhuland formed the company in 1900, taking over the work of the David Smith and John Young shipyards that had earlier thrived further west on the waterfront. They at first produced sailing vessels but, by the late Twenties, most vessels were built with auxiliary power. In the Thirties and Forties production turned to diesel powered vessels of all types. By 1976, when the shipyard was sold to Scotia Trawler Ltd., Smith & Rhuland had built 279 commercial vessels and 107 yachts and pleasure boats.*

INTRODUCTION

*Absurd and outrageous as these people are in their dispositions I must yet do them
ye Justice to observe that they are indefatigable when labouring for themselves. Most
of them are well under cover. All of them have gardens and many of them have good
framed houses. They have cut on ye whole a Considerable quantity of hay. They are
acquainted with ye Country for 10 miles round; and the more they know of it the
better they seem to like it; insomuch that if they go on as they have begun, and no
forward circumstances put them wrong, they must, I think, in spite of themselves,
become a flourishing people, and fulfil to ye public every expectation
formed concerning them.*

—Excerpt of a letter from Colonel Charles Lawrence to Governor Hopson
of Nova Scotia, dated 8 August 1753, regarding the Lunenburg settlers.

LUNENBURG was established in June 1753 and was
the first permanent British colonial settlement in Nova Scotia
outside of Halifax and Annapolis Royal. The settlers were
German speaking "foreign Protestants," deliberately recruited by the British to counterbalance the presence of the
roughly 10,000 Acadians who already lived in Nova Scotia.
The British were in the latter stages of their long struggle
with France for control of the Canadian colonies. Halifax had
been established four years earlier to counteract the French
fortress at Louisbourg. The Acadians, descendants of earlier
French settlers, wished to remain neutral in the conflict but
were perceived by the British as a threat. The "foreign
Protestants" were recruited because they were thought to be
more reliable and hard-working than the "industrial poor" of
Britain, and because they could be counted on to be loyal to
the British Crown. Lunenburg, formerly known as Merliguish,
was chosen as the best site for the new settlement because
it was only "16 leagues distant" from Halifax, situated in a
defensible location on a good harbour, and already had
about 300 acres of cleared land.

After assembling in Halifax (some for up to two years
beforehand), the 1,453 settlers were transported to
Lunenburg in small ships. Most had undertaken to pay for
their passage from Europe by labouring on public works, and
they were, at first, encamped in tents while helping to build
blockhouses, defensive pickets, and storehouses. Once these
projects were under way, each family was allocated 500 feet
of boards and 250 nails with which to begin construction of

185/191 TOWNSEND STREET – C1883/1885

*Two houses built by John Maxner, a boat builder and
house builder, in the late 1880s.*

7 York Street — late 1700s

An early Cape Cod house of "coulisse" construction. The section to the left of the door was the original "half cape" house, which had no cellar. The section to the right was added later and included cellar space giving access to a dug well. The old well is now filled in and the building sits on a modern foundation.

their own houses. According to Lunenburg County historian Mather B. DesBrisay, the first temporary houses were "constructed of round poles, and were about 6 feet in the post, and 18 or 20 feet square outside. Others were of hewed timber, about 6 inches through. The roofs of many were thatched. The doors and shutters were of 2-inch plank, when it could be had, and fastened with iron bolts."

The town site was laid out on a rectangular grid, in accordance with the standard British "model plan" for colonial settlements. Superimposed on the steep hillside overlooking the harbour, the grid consisted of six divisions of eight blocks, with each block subdivided into fourteen lots, and each lot 40 feet wide by 60 feet deep. The streets were laid out parallel and perpendicular to the harbour, and a four-block area in the centre of the grid was reserved as a public parade ground. Areas to the east and west of the town site were reserved as common land. Garden lots were laid out further to the east, and 30-acre farm lots were laid out to the north, west, and south. Each settler was allocated a town lot, a garden lot, and a farm lot. Inland areas beyond the immediate environs of the town were surveyed over the succeeding twelve years, and farms and

woodlots were eventually granted (in 1784) to those who had cleared and cultivated them. In its entirety, Lunenburg Township comprised 180,000 acres and formed the foundation of the settlement of present day Lunenburg County, with Lunenburg as the shire town.

The "model plan" established the urban form of Lunenburg from its earliest days. The small size of the lots and the orientation of the grid predetermined that houses would be built close to each other, close to the street, and parallel to the harbour. The varied topography created a situation in which houses would overlook each other on hilly sites. The parade ground provided a site for public buildings. The area between the lower street (Montague Street) and the shore provided for development of wharves and warehouses.

The first permanent houses were built in what is now known as the "Cape Cod" style—small, wooden houses with a compact floor plan, two or three rooms on the ground floor, a sleeping loft, a massive central chimney, small windows, and a steeply pitched, gable or gambrel roof to shed rain and snow. The Cape Cod had developed over the previous 150 years in the New England colonies as an adaptation of older British building forms to the harsh winter climate and available building materials of the American northeast; it was adopted in colonial Nova Scotia for the same practical reasons. Many of the Lunenburg settlers would have been introduced to the Cape Cod style during their two-year wait in Halifax, and it can be imagined that they seized upon it as a sensible way of replacing their first temporary shelters with permanent homes.

While the style was colonial, the construction method used by the Lunenburgers was their own. Instead of conventional post and beam framing, they used a technique known as "coulisse" construction, in which walls were constructed of solid 3-inch planks, slotted, one above the other, into massive grooved corner posts, and secured with spikes or wooden pegs (trenails). The timber walls were then covered with weatherboards or shingles on the exterior and finishing boards on the interior. This technique was rooted in the wooden building traditions of medieval Europe and was rarely used elsewhere in colonial North America. A number of buildings of coulisse construction are still standing in Lunenburg to this day.

As the town developed over the succeeding decades, larger, two-storey houses were built in the British Neo-Classical (Georgian) style, using braced, post and beam framing, and placing greater emphasis on architectural style and proportion. These houses had a more formal, centre hall plan and a five-bay facade, with pairs of matching windows arranged symmetrically on either side of a central door. Windows were multi-paned and the door was usually framed by sidelights and a transom window. Exterior trim was more elaborate than on the Cape Cod houses but remained conservative.

By the early nineteenth century, the architectural tone of Lunenburg was well established. In 1830, Captain William Moorsom, a military engineer, visited the town and reported that the houses "are almost all of wood, constructed with a view to comfort rather than appearance." He also noted that "every house-holder from the highest to the lowest, appears to possess the means of keeping his tenement in repair and good order ... [and that] ... a whimsical taste has introduced the custom of painting the exterior white, red, pink, and even green...."

The "foreign Protestants" were originally farming people, and in the early years of the settlement, they gained their livelihood principally from the land, supplying wood and farm produce to Halifax. Over the course of time, however, they turned to the sea and developed a thriving economy based on shipbuilding, fishing, and commerce. Lucrative trade opportunities opened up after the American Revolution, when ports in the British West Indies were closed to American vessels. Lunenburgers were quick to capitalize by exporting the products of Lunenburg Township—lumber, shingles, staves, and pickled and dried fish—in return for rum, molasses, sugar, and coffee. By 1829, the town had about 100 vessels engaged in coastal trade, foreign trade, and fishing, and there were twenty-two stores stocked with British and West India goods. Further trade opened up in 1839, when the town was declared a Free Port.

At first, the fishing fleet was quite small, with fishermen operating in the inshore waters of the coast of Nova Scotia, the Gulf of St. Lawrence, and the coast of Labrador. In 1767, there were only six fishing boats.

125 PELHAM STREET – c1793

A Georgian house with a formal, five-bay facade in the British Classical tradition. Built for Benjamin Knaut, a merchant and early sheriff of Lunenburg.

By 1811, the number had risen to about twenty, but by 1850, it had declined to about ten (according to Captain Benjamin Anderson's recollections, recorded by DesBrisay). Between the 1850s and 1870s, however, a number of innovations were made that resulted in a major expansion of fishing and shipbuilding. The method of fishing changed from handlining to trawling, thus bringing in larger catches; the attention of the fishermen turned to the rich, offshore banks of the continental shelf; and larger vessels were built, enabling longer trips to be made. The first Lunenburg vessel to venture out to the Grand Banks was the schooner *Union,* owned by Zwicker and Company, in 1856. Others followed, including Captain Anderson in the *Dielytris,* in 1873, and, by the late 1870s and early 1880s, there were about 150 schooners fishing out of Lunenburg County, with almost one half of these based in Lunenburg town.

Lunenburg shipbuilders developed the "salt-banker"—a 100-foot, 100-ton wooden schooner with a large sail area, a large, open deck for stacking dories and gear, and a large hold for storing salted fish. Fishing vessels were built and outfitted on a share basis (sixty-four shares) and the profits from fishing trips were divided proportionately among the shareholders.

46 LORNE STREET – LATE 1880S

A typical, late nineteenth-century Lunenburg-style house with an extended dormer connected to a lower porch. This view is from the rear. There is an identical centre bay on the front of the house. Built in the New Town for William Gaetz, a fisherman.

Founding families, such as the Zwickers and Rudolfs, initially dominated the business but, in the 1860s and 1870s, other firms, such as those of James D. Eisenhauer and Lewis Anderson entered the field and began outfitting their own vessels and developing new wharves and warehouses. The expansions in the fishing and shipbuilding industries stimulated the town's economy, and by the 1880s, the waterfront was a hive of activity, filled with shipyards and the workshops of blacksmiths, block makers, sail makers and riggers, and the warehouses and curing sheds of the fishing companies.

By 1862, the population of Lunenburg had grown sufficiently that expansion beyond the Old Town was necessary. An area of common land to the west was laid out in building lots, to become known as the New Town, and an area extending east along Pelham Street (the road to Garden Lots) was also laid out.

In the 1870s, the prosperity generated by the fishery began to show in changes to the town's architecture. Many of the old Cape Cod and Georgian houses were renovated with larger windows, new roof dormers, new entrance porches, and elaborate trim around windows and doors. Pattern books describing the popular, mid-Victorian architectural "revivals" were readily available, and Lunenburg home owners and builders could choose from styles such as Gothic Revival (which emphasized peaked, centre-gable dormers); Greek Revival (which used pedimented gables, wooden pilasters, and built-up mouldings to simulate the classical Greek temple); the Italianate style (which emphasized rounded windows and bracketed cornices); and the French Second Empire style (with its characteristic mansard roof, bay windows, and projecting towers). New construction techniques, particularly "balloon" framing, which was lighter than earlier post and beam framing, enabled these more fanciful buildings to be erected, and advances in woodworking technology made machine-sawn brackets and decorative mouldings readily available.

Instead of faithfully following the pattern books, however, Lunenburgers came up with their own variations and were particularly creative when it came to the design of dormers. In what might now be viewed as a rather inspired way, they took the popular five-sided "Scottish" dormer and extended it outward, upward, and downward to create what has since become referred to as the "Lunenburg Bump"—a quirky, vernacular feature that eventually became the architectural hallmark of the town. The builders combined the "Bump" with porches, verandas, towers, widow's walks, bay windows, and decorative millwork in an almost endless variety of ways. By the end of the 1880s, they had transformed Lunenburg into an eclectic and idiosyncratic architectural showpiece, a place recognizably different from all other Nova Scotian towns.

Few of the Lunenburg builders had any formal architectural training, yet between them, they created what is now recognized as a unique regional architectural style. Many, such as Joseph and Solomon Morash, also designed boats. Others, such as John and James Maxner, were boat builders who occasionally built houses. C. Albert Smith built houses but also ran a planing mill, where he produced "doors, sashes, window frames, door frames, balusters, and all kinds of mouldings...." In many cases, houses were designed and built by their owners without professional assistance. It was this diverse mix of skills and practical knowledge, combined with the "shipbuilder's eye,"

321 LINCOLN STREET – 1877

A late nineteenth-century, high-style Lunenburg house with a complex, multi-faceted frontispiece and decorative millwork. Built for Charles Smith, a mariner and merchant who ran a store from a building behind the house.

and no doubt, a good dose of the "absurd and outrageous" Lunenburg disposition that produced the distinct architecture that we see today.

By 1888, when it was officially incorporated, the town was well established as the administrative, religious, educational, and mercantile centre of Lunenburg County, and was home to a good number of public buildings. St. John's Anglican Church, the second oldest Anglican church in Canada, had been standing since 1754. The Presbyterian, Lutheran, Methodist, Catholic, and Baptist congregations also had fine church buildings. The courthouse (now the Anglican church hall) had been standing more or less in its original form since 1775. The first Lunenburg Academy, originally built in 1865, was still standing in the central square. (It later burned down and was replaced by the present Academy on Gallows Hill in 1895.) The railway came to town in the late 1870s and was extended along the waterfront in the 1880s. The first Fire Hall was built in 1889. The Town Hall was built in 1893. Lincoln Street, the main commercial street, had a vibrant mix of two- and three-storey buildings, with shop fronts at street level and residences, rooms, and meeting halls on the upper storeys. The town was in its heyday in the midst of what the Lunenburg Progress Enterprise called, in 1897, "a boom of splendid proportions."

Unlike its houses, the town's public buildings were generally designed by architects, although even then, in most cases, local carpenter-builders were closely involved. St. John's Anglican Church, for example, one of the most outstanding early churches in Canada, was "Gothicized" in the 1870s on the basis of designs by the Halifax architect David Stirling. It underwent further Gothic transformations in the 1890s under the direction of Joseph and Solomon Morash. The Morash brothers also supervised construction of the Lunenburg Academy, designed by the Saint John architect Harry Mott. The Town Hall, unusual in Lunenburg because of its brick construction, was designed by the architect Henry Busch. The Merchants Bank (now the Royal Bank) was also a masonry building and was designed by Sydney Dumaresq.

The fishing and shipbuilding boom continued into the early twentieth century with new firms such as W. C. Smith & Co. (the precursor of the present day National Sea Products) and Adams and Knickle (which also still exists) building new warehouses and refurbishing old ones. The Smith and Rhuland shipyard was established in 1900. The Lunenburg Foundry and the Lunenburg Marine Railway were also both established in this period, broadening the range of marine services in the town.

New houses continued to be built, but styles were changing. The Queen Anne style, with its large bay windows, expansive verandas, and corner turrets was favoured by some wealthy citizens. People of more modest means tended to choose the simpler, hip-roofed, Four Square style. The turn-of-the-century houses were less extravagant and more restrained in style than those of previous decades but were still compatible in scale, form, and materials. On Lincoln Street, several new commercial buildings were constructed including the Capitol Theatre, built in 1907.

After World War I, Lunenburg maintained its position as a leader in the fishery by again adjusting to changing technology and economic conditions. In the early twenties, the traditional salt fishery continued to thrive, with fast schooners, such as the *Bluenose* (built by Smith & Rhuland in 1921), efficiently supplying the companies. By the late twenties, diesel-powered trawlers began to displace the sailing fleet, and production turned from salt fish to frozen and processed fish. W. C. Smith & Co. (by then transformed into Lunenburg Sea Products) pioneered this change in 1927 by sending the first beam trawler, the *Geraldine,* to the offshore banks, and by setting up cold storage facilities, a cannery, and a fish meal plant to supply the changing market.

During the Depression, the demand for fish declined, and the town was not immune to the widespread hard times. Even so, some Lunenburgers demonstrated their ongoing adaptability (and their continuing tradition of trade with the West Indies) by running liquor to the United States in high-speed, Lunenburg-built "Rum Runners," such as the famous *I'm Alone.*

After World War II, the fishery revived and the companies, particularly the newly formed National Sea Products, embarked upon a new era of industrialized fish processing, using radio, radar, and sonar technology, and larger trawlers and draggers. By the late 1950s, National Sea's fish plant occupied the entire western half of the Old Town waterfront. Shipbuilding continued at the Smith & Rhuland yard with production of fishing vessels, freighters, pleasure craft, and special purpose boats, including replicas of the *Bounty* (1960) and the *Bluenose II* (1963).

In 1965, National Sea Products opened a new plant outside the town boundary and left its old plant empty. Instead of seeing this as a crisis, the community recognized the potential of the abandoned building. By adapting yet again to challenging circumstances, they began a process of converting the old plant into a museum—the Fisheries Museum of the Atlantic.

Today, Lunenburg is still very much the "Fishing Capital of Canada," with the traditional industries of fishing, shipbuilding, ship repair, and ship outfitting providing the foundation of the economy. But it has also adjusted to the economic realities of the late twentieth century by successfully embracing tourism. The Fisheries Museum now attracts over 100,000 visitors a year. Along with it have grown dozens of small, tourist-oriented businesses and several major community festivals built around local crafts, folk music, and German "Oktoberfest" activities (in addition to the long-standing annual Fisheries Exhibition and Fishermen's Reunion). The town's historic architecture provides a unifying backdrop to all these tourism activities, and the importance of architectural conservation is now widely recognized by the Town Council, volunteer groups such as the Lunenburg Heritage Society, and many individual property owners. Most of the latter still take considerable pride in keeping their "tenements in repair," and in recent years, some have taken the further step of restoring buildings to their original character.

In 1991, the Old Town was designated a National Historic District on the basis of the integrity of its town plan, the cohesiveness in its architecture, and the continuity in its historical themes. This designation is a recognition that Lunenburg today is a living, breathing, working historic town, where the past can be tangibly felt in houses and waterfront buildings; in churches and public buildings; in stores and streets and open spaces; and in the ongoing lives and livelihoods of its citizens, many of whom are direct descendants of the original "foreign Protestant" settlers.

If Colonel Charles Lawrence were alive today, he could take considerable satisfaction in knowing that his intuition was correct—the Lunenburgers, "indefatigable when labouring for themselves" have, indeed, become the "flourishing people" that he predicted, and their town, which began as a small cluster of "good framed houses" on the shores of Merliguish Harbour, has become, after 250 years, one of the most outstanding historic communities in North America.

Bill Plaskett
Halifax, October 1995

ADAMS & KNICKLE WHAREHOUSE – C1870S

A complex of waterfront buildings representing the evolution of the Lunenburg fishery. The steep gable-roofed buildings were built by James D. Eisenhauer & Co. in the 1860s and 1870s. The section at the rear with the shallower pitched roofed was added about 1917, when the Eisenhauer business was taken over by the Lunenburg Outfitting Company. Adams & Knickle acquired the buildings in 1943 and added the shed roofed section on the right about 1959.

MOST TRAVELLERS coming to Lunenburg for the first time begin by visiting the Fisheries Museum of the Atlantic. As they climb out of their cars and stretch, their gaze moves along the museum wharves and then up the town's steep slope. Lunenburg seems to press down upon the waterfront, street stacked upon street, a thousand windows staring out to the harbour. For a moment, the visitor feels the town's gaze in the way that returning fishermen do when they return to port.

This sense of being perched over waterfront and harbour is felt most keenly along Montague and Pelham streets. Walking along these lower streets, one's attention is continually seduced by irresistible views. The harbour front's proximity also has shaped the character of these streets, mixing fine residences with old, commercial buildings, the latter serving marine industry, the fishery, and now tourism.

The new sidewalks and asphalt of the lowermost street, Bluenose Drive, are a recent development. In previous years, this stretch of waterfront contained a grittier bustle as trucks and forklifts bounced over rail-road tracks and scurried along dirt service roads. Marine enterprise has endured, and a stroll eastward along Bluenose Drive and further along the eastern end of Montague provides intriguing glimpses of wharves, warehouses, and waterfront shops.

At the very end of Montague, one arrives at the "Shipyards" where Smith & Rhuland Ltd. (sold to Scotia Trawlers Ltd. in 1976) built many of Lunenburg's saltbank schooners and other vessels, including the original *Bluenose* in 1921; the replica HMS *Bounty* in 1960; the replica *Bluenose II* in 1963; and the replica HMS *Rose* in 1970. Beyond the Scotia Trawlers shops is the Lunenburg Marine Railway, crucial to the town's marine service industry. A small park on Pelham provides a vantage from which to view the Marine Railway and the Shipyards.

Pelham is one of Lunenburg's longest residential streets and offers several of the town's most appealing streetscapes. If time for a walk is limited, Pelham Street provides a good sampling of Lunenburg's main architectural themes.

ABOVE: *The* Theresa E. Connor, *a restored Lunenburg "salt-banker," is one of the main attractions at the Fisheries Museum. The vessel is open to the public above and below deck and illustrates the working environment of the banks fishermen. The dories on the wharf were the type used for setting and hauling trawl. The building on the left was originally the Lunenburg Sea Products Ice House. The building on the right was built about 1899 by W.C. Smith & Co. and, over the years, has been used as a salt fish warehouse, a cooperage, and a fish packing plant.*

LEFT: *The Fisheries Museum of the Atlantic occupies the former National Sea Products fish plant. The hatch roofed buildings at the foot of Cornwallis Street were constructed about 1945 and were originally used as coal sheds and for general storage. The vessel at the wharf is the steel-hulled side trawler* Cape Sable. *Cornwallis Street climbs the hill behind the Museum, with houses rising in tiers along the cross streets. The spires of Zion Lutheran Church and St. John's Anglican Church can be seen at the top of the hill.*

170 MONTAGUE STREET — 1897

Adams and Knickle entered the salt fish business in 1897. In 1942 they acquired the assets of the Lunenburg Outfitting Company and later those of Acadian Supplies Ltd. Today the firm is engaged in the scallop fishery. Their gambrel-roofed warehouse and store was built by Joseph and Solomon Morash. On the front facade it has ashlar imitation cladding– wooden boards cut and planed to resemble squared stone blocks laid in regular courses. The sides of the building are shingled. The canopy over the storefront was added in the early 1990s as part of a film set.

For one hundred years, the railway ran along the Lunenburg waterfront behind the houses, stores, and warehouses of Montague Street, terminating at the government wharf. The tracks were removed in the late 1980s to make way for construction and paving of Bluenose Drive–the Old Town's newest street. Waterfront buildings were always kept brightly painted–different colours identifying the premises of the various firms. The blue building on the left was built about 1873 for Lewis Anderson & Co. and is now part of the Deep Sea Trawlers Division of Clearwater Atlantic Ltd. The Adams & Knickle buildings are distinguished by their bright red paint. In this photo, three painters are returning home in the afternoon sun after a day on the job.

140 PELHAM STREET — c1860s

Over its one hundred and fifty-year history, this building has served as a workshop for blacksmiths, coopers, and carriage makers and has been used as a flour and feed warehouse and a coal supply warehouse. It is presently used as an oil distibution depot. The way that the building is fitted to the slope of Pelham Street is particularly interesting, and its panelled, round-headed, warehouse doors are unique in the town.

152/146 Montague Street — late 1880s

Until 1972, when it ceased operations, Zwicker and Company was the oldest fishing company in Canada in continuous operation. It was also, with the exception of the Hudson's Bay Company, one of the longest lived privately-owned companies in the country. Founded in 1789, to export fish, lumber, and staves to the West Indies, the company pioneered the change from the inshore to the offshore fishery in 1856, when it sent the schooner Union to the Grand Banks. This building and the smaller one next door were the company's headquarters. The infill addition was constructed in 1978.

55 MONTAGUE STREET – c1876

Joseph and Solomon Morash were two of Lunenburg's most prolific builders in the late nineteenth-century. This was their own house–a bell-cast, hipped gambrel-roofed structure, built into the hillside in typical Lunenburg fashion, and presenting an elaborate, symmetrical facade to Montague Street. In 1977, it was purchased by the Lunenburg Heritage Society and restored as a demonstration project. It is now operated commercially as the "Morash Gallery."

53 MONTAGUE STREET — c1860

When this graceful, Italianate frontispiece was added to George Anderson's house in the 1880s, it had a third storey with a bell-cast roof, peak-roofed lookout windows, and a domed cap. The house is one of five Anderson houses on this block built by the descendants of the Loyalist John Anderson, who came to Lunenburg in 1793 from Philadelphia. Between them, the family operated a blacksmith shop, a boat-building business, a tailor shop and a farm outside the town.

28 PELHAM STREET – C1877

John Anderson built this modified French Second Empire style house about 1877 for $1589.98. He ran a boat-building business on the waterfront below the property and engaged actively in the public affairs of the town. The finishing touches that he made to the house can still be appreciated today, particularly the bracketted, dentilled eaves, the unusual round-headed dormer, and the graceful, curved mouldings over the windows and main door.

36 PELHAM STREET — C1828

*The "Maple Bird Anderson" house is set into the hill-
side on a granite foundation. In the lower storey
there are two open fireplaces with bake ovens and
original ironware. The extended dormer was added
in the 1880s. The "cocks comb" roof cresting and
finial are highlighted in the afternoon sun.*

56 Pelham Street – c1875

Lunenburg's hillside setting enabled houses to be built with a front entrance facing the street and a full, lower storey and rear entrance on the downill side. This is illustrated particularly well by the Henry Gaetz House, at the corner of Pelham and Cornwallis streets.

54/52 PELHAM STREET – C1860/1900

*Both houses in this photo trace back into the Anderson family,
who built all of the houses on this block. Fifty-four Pelham
was the home of Charles Anderson. Built step-fashion into the
hillside, it was originally a simple, gable-roofed structure. The
Lunenburg Bump was added in the 1880s. Charles ran a tailor
shop in a small building next door, which was replaced about
1900 by the hipped-gable roofed house built by his son,
Charles A. Anderson, also a tailor. Also shown in the photo is
part of the barn on the adjacent property, which was owned
by Charles senior's brother, William, who was known as
"Farmer" Anderson.*

82 PELHAM STREET — C1774

*The Romkey House, one of Lunenburg's oldest buildings, once
served as the town's Customs Office. The gambrel roofed
house has solid plank walls and an up-and-down board roof.
It is reputed to have originally been thatched.*

75 PELHAM STREET — LATE 1880S .

*"Duff" Kaulback was the grandson of John Henry Kaulback,
an early sheriff of Lunenburg, and great-grandson of Martin
von Kaulback, who came from Germany with the first settlers.
His family name is inscribed on the entrance step of this
grand, French Second Empire style house.*

15 KING STREET – C1829

Home to the Zwicker family for more than 120 years, this house was originally built in the Georgian style, with traditional five-bay fenestration. The Zwickers were one of the town's most prominent merchant families and they were one of the first to Victorianize their house when the fisheries expanded in the 1870s. By 1879, the original smaller windows had been replaced by large ones, and this three-tiered, Italianate frontispiece had been added.

120 PELHAM STREET – 1923

The old Masonic Temple is remarkable on two counts–it is the only overtly Greek Revival building in Lunenburg, and it was built in 1923, well into the twentieth-century. Its graceful classical facade accurately reflects the manner of the Greek Revival style, with six Ionic pilasters "supporting" a simplified entablature and pediment. The building is tucked away on Pelham Street, behind the Bank of Montreal, and is easy to miss. Its formal front elevation is best viewed head on in the late afternoon, when the low angle light reveals its subtle texture.

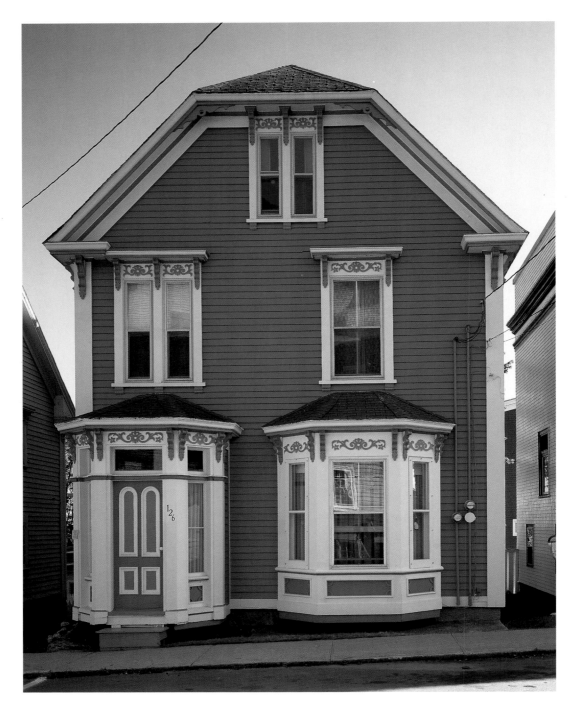

126 PELHAM STREET — C1880

The quirky asymmetry of this house is highlighted by a meticulous paint scheme. Built by master carpenters Joseph and Solomon Morash for J. Moyle Rudolf, the house sold for $2,454.74 in 1883.

138 PELHAM STREET — 1880S

*Edwin Bailly, a blacksmith, built this house on the site of an
earlier house that he moved over onto the lot next door (and
which still stands in a much altered form). For the frontispiece on
his new house he chose this boxy, Italianate Bump, the proportions of which are emphasized here in the late afternoon sun.*

178 & 172 Pelham Street — 1880s

These double-bay houses establish a strong architectural rhythm along the south side of Pelham Street. The one on the left was built for Captain Simeon Hebb about 1884, the other for William Smith about 1883. The gambrel-roofed house on the right was built about 1899 by James Geldert and was used as a store from the 1920s to the 1950s.

230 PELHAM STREET – c1897

Paired Tuscan columns support the veranda roof on the old
James Holland house, and a tasteful paint scheme highlights
bracketted cornices. Double-bay windows echo those on the
house next door, which was built about ten years earlier by
Peter Bichard, a fisherman.

OLD TOWN:
THE MIDDLE STREETS

ALTHOUGH OLD TOWN'S essential character was shaped by the harbour and the sea, town life has been defined by other factors as well, such as the overlay of the eighteenth-century British model-town plat upon a sloping terrain. Near the centre of this grid, the middle streets—Lincoln and Cumberland—are central axes in much of Lunenburg's activity. Another axis, King Street, bisects the middle streets and the other east-west streets as it runs north from the harbour.

Lincoln Street is the location of Lunenburg's principal retail shopping district. Few towns have avoided the pressure of outlying shopping malls, but Lunenburg has. The vitality of Lincoln Street is an essential ingredient in town life. With its western end extending towards New Town, Lincoln possesses a number of retail premises, including many that are architecturally distinctive, along its western blocks. East of King Street, Lincoln offers one of Lunenburg's most notable residential streetscapes. Within the historic district, virtually all businesses are located either on or below Lincoln and Cumberland.

Cumberland Street is the final east-west street in Old Town's sharp rise from the harbour. For the most part, the district's northern rise begins to slacken above Cumberland. Cumberland also borders the area originally set forth in the town plan as a central parade ground. Approximately one-half of the original four-block area is still community green space: either on the grounds of St. John's Anglican Church or in the park areas on either side of the Town Hall.

Standing before the town War Memorial where Cumberland crosses King, one can almost look straight down King Street to the harbour. This 80-foot wide avenue descending to the harbour is a central feature of British colonial town planning. Despite the fact that Lunenburg is one of the finest intact examples of the eighteenth-century model plan, the grand intention of the original design was frustrated more than one-and-one-half centuries ago by the truncation of the avenue with development along Montague. This change to design speaks to the practical, flexible outlook of Lunenburg's citizens.

87 LINCOLN STREET – C1884

Carpenter J. Rufus Oxner used carved, thistle-motif brackets to join the doorway and the projecting dormer on this house that he built in 1884. Today, as you drive by on Lincoln Street, you have to slow down and look up to see them.

RIGHT: CORNWALLIS STREET

Lunenburg's grid layout created streets parallel and perpendicular to the harbour. Here, Cornwallis Street crosses Lincoln, and marches on down to the water.

KAULBACK BLOCK – c1900

Charles Edwin Kaulback was one of Lunenburg's largest ship and real estate owners and there were few financial enterprises in the town in which he did not have an interest. He lived in the house on the right, which was built about 1860 and Victorianized in the 1890s. At the turn of the century, he built the office block on the left, incorporating some older buildings that had previously stood on the site. Today, the Kaulback Block is one of the first buildings that you notice when driving into the Old Town along Lincoln Street.

156-166 LINCOLN STREET

On one hand, Lunenburg buildings are unified by similarities of scale, height, proportion, and facade detail; on the other, the differences between them create a whole variety of interesting rhythms and patterns. In this view of buildings on Lincoln Street, the storefront windows and cornices line up with each other, while the second floor windows and overall building heights have a surprising, up-down-up-down, 3-2-3-2 rhythm. The building with the "boomtown" facade was the office of the N.S. Telephone Company from 1906-1931.

183 LINCOLN STREET — 1905

Lewis Hirtle was a photographer who left a valuable visual record of turn-of-the-century Lunenburg. This was his shop and studio. Johnny Knickle carried on the business in the 1920s and Wilf Eisnor runs it today as "Knickle's Studio."

28 KING STREET – C1876

Facing the broad avenue of King Street in the centre of Lunenburg, this house was the home of the town's first mayor, Augustus Wolff. Built by Nicolas Berringer, it has an eccentric design where the symmetry of the dormers and chimneys is counterbalanced by the off-centre alignment of the lower windows.

306 Lincoln Street — 1905

*This house was built for J.W. McLachlan, a dry goods merchant
and former Registrar of Births and Deaths. It features Lunenburg's
only octagonal corner tower. The veranda and exterior staircase,
which has a certain "ship's bridge" quality about it, was reconstructed in 1993, based on old photographs.*

315 LINCOLN STREET – c1876

Situated on the brow of the hill, the Italianate features of the old Henry Wilson house are cast in a dramatic perspective. Henry ran a boot and shoe store on Lincoln Street, had shares in Lunenburg fishing vessels, and also developed the Pelham Street property on which the Lunenburg Royal Bank (formerly the Merchants Bank) now stands. Henry's son, Morris Wilson, was president of the Royal Bank from 1934-1946.

321/325/331 LINCOLN STREET

*The interesting thing about Lunenburg houses is the balance
that is struck between their similarities and their differences.
Here, in one of the town's most intact, historic streetscapes,
three houses have underlying similarities of form, facade
arrangement, and relationship to the street, combined with
clearly stated differences of detail, accent, and interpretation.
The house on the left was built about 1877 for Charles Smith;
the one in the middle about 1886 for Daniel Rudolf, the
town's second mayor; the one on the right, about 1877, for
Capt. James Hunt.*

REAR, 170 CUMBERLAND STREET — c1888

Lunenburg's layout of small lots and narrow streets often creates surprising views of the backs of houses on the next street. This house fronts on Cumberland Street, but can be seen from Lincoln. It was built by James Morash, a ships carpenter, and has identical projecting bays on the front and rear.

331 LINCOLN STREET — C1877

*The archetypal Lunenburg house: 1½ storeys high; built into a
slight slope to create a tall front facade requiring a few steps
up to the entrance; a central frontispiece comprised of a projecting five-sided dormer over a rectangular porch; wide cornerboards framing a clapboard exterior; high eaves; window hoods
wide enough to catch the afternoon light and reflect it up to
the bracketted eaves overhang. Built for Captain James Hunt.*

35 HOPSON STREET — c1876

Many old Lunenburg houses are built right to the street line. On this house, at the corner of Cumberland and Hopson streets, the projecting dormer overhangs the sidewalk. The owner has chosen a paint scheme that distinguishes the trim from the clapboard wall surface, but leaves it to form alone to define the brackets under the eave returns and the scrollsawn filigree on the lintels.

UNITED CHURCH — 1883/85

Of the six old church buildings in Lunenburg, the United Church (formerly Methodist) is the largest. Built over a two-year period between 1883 and 1885, it faces the south side of the Parade Square and replaced an earlier church on the north side of the square. Size appears to have been a matter of great concern to the early Methodist congregation. DesBrisay records that the earlier church was sawn in half in 1865 to enable an extra ten feet to be added to the middle, and that, in 1871, a further twenty feet was added. He also records that, when the new church was opened in 1885, "fully fifteen hundred [people] were accommodated in the spacious edifice ... [listening to an] ... appropriate sermon ... by Rev. J.J. Teasdale." The church spire was at one time a towering 75 feet high but was later truncated and covered with the bell-cast, copper-roofed cap that is seen today. The design of the church is particularly interesting in the way that the massive form of the building is visually tied to the ground by the darkness of the three doors and the finishing flourish of curved picket fences on either side.

BOSCAWEN INN — C1888

Dramatically situated on a steep site overlooking Lincoln Street, "Boscawen Manor" was commissioned by Senator H.A.N. Kaulback, one of the most influential (and wealthy) figures in Lunenburg's history, for his daughter, Edna, and her husband, James Rudolf, as a wedding gift. Designed by architect Henry Busch, who also designed the Lunenburg Town Hall, the Zion Lutheran Church, and the Halifax Public Gardens Bandstand, it is Lunenburg's best example of the Queen Anne Revival style. It has been used as a hotel since 1945.

Town Hall — 1891/93

Described variously as a "sober interpretation" of the Second Empire style and as a "boldly detailed" building, the Town Hall and Courthouse was designed by architect Henry Busch, Nova Scotia's foremost exponent of the style during the late 19th-century. It was built amidst controversy over whether a new County Courthouse should be built in Lunenburg or in the nearby rival town of Bridgewater. Construction was doggedly commenced in both towns before the disagreement was resolved in 1893 by the "Act to Settle Difficulties That Have Arisen With Regard to the Courthouse in the County of Lunenburg," which decreed that court sessions would be held alternately in both towns. The building is unusual in the town because of its brick construction. Aside from the replacement of the original slate roof with asphalt shingles, the removal of the original clock tower and roof cresting, a few minor alter-ations to doors, and the recent addition of a metal fire escape at the rear, the building is substantially intact in its original style.

65 CUMBERLAND STREET – C1775

This building was the first Lunenburg Courthouse. It originally had an entrance and a large Gothic dormer set in the centre of its long elevation, facing the western end of the Parade Square. The building was vacated in 1893 when the Court moved to the newly built Town Hall. In 1902, it was purchased by St. John's Anglican Church for use as a Parish Hall. Subsequently, the old dormer was taken off, the main door was relocated to the north end (photo right), and the building was lengthened by two window bays on the south end (photo centre). In 1964, a large addition was made on the western side (photo left) in the same style as the original, with hooded, lancet windows, clapboard siding, wide cornerboards, and a new main entrance. The interior of the building still bears the mark of its original use in the form of a large wall mural depicting a Royal Coat of Arms and the inscription "Fiat Justitia ruat caelum" (Let Justice be done though heaven fall).

116 CUMBERLAND STREET – C1858

This Bump was added to the underlying Cape Cod structure in the 1880s by Isaac Zinck, a fisherman, who owned the property from 1874 until 1926. The house is one of four in the town where the enlarged dormer is supported by posts.

70 CUMBERLAND STREET — C1841

Facing the central Parade Square, this house was built by ship-builder John Young for Joshua Kaulback, a merchant, who conducted his business on the premises. In 1871, the house was passed on to his nephew, Captain Ephraim Oxner, who owned it only a short time before he was lost at sea in 1875. It later succeeded to S. Watson Oxner, who carried on the family business and became Mayor of Lunenburg from 1891 to 1894. The house remained in the Oxner family until 1983. Documentary records suggest that the cannon in front of the house was used to scare off an American privateer at Lower La Have (eight miles from Lunenburg) during the 1780s, and was acquired through Ephraim Oxner's mother, Anna B. Oxner. It was placed at the corner to keep horse and ox-drawn vehicles from sliding against the house. The house is one of the most graceful, neo-classical houses in the Old Town and it is interesting to see how it retains its poise, despite the asymmetrical position of the dormer (a later addition).

TOWNSEND is the first east-west street lying north of Old Town's original four-block parade ground. Lunenburg's first church, St. John's Anglican, occupies the old parade ground's westernmost block and seems to sit at the very heart of Lunenburg, tying together its upper and lower districts. Beyond Townsend are Fox, York, Lawrence, and Creighton streets. Approximately one half of the forty-eight-block area set forth in the plat of 1753 is bounded by Townsend and Creighton.

Strolling along these upper streets, one becomes aware that the steep northern rise from the harbour has substantially levelled. The upper district is situated in an east-west saddle, with the Lunenburg Academy atop a gentle rise to the west. Blockhouse Hill commands the summit of a much more abrupt slope, which climbs east from Hopson Street. Lunenburg's principal fortifications occupied these two elevated positions in the town's early years.

With few exceptions, the upper streets are noncommerical. They comprise a district of houses, churches, and, of course, the Lunenburg Academy, which dominates the town's skyline. Perhaps the best plan for exploring these streets is to simply follow one's fancy. From numerous locations, the towers of the Academy and the steeples of St. John's, St. Andrew's, St. Norbert's, and Zion Evangelical Lutheran churches all beckon. Adjacent to the churches and the school, there are numerous residential blocks.

Although most houses in Old Town's upper district have origins in the eighteenth or nineteenth century, there is no easily discernible correlation between street locations and architectural eras. Instead, there is a delightful juxtaposition of architectural types as well as frequent overlaying of one era's style upon another. It is a pleasure to roam this upper district, searching out each building's likely story from the layers of form; noting the repeated occurrences of different builders' signatures; all the while accompanied by the murmur of town life stirring in these crowded old streets.

126 FOX STREET – 1888

In this photo, the juxtaposition of granite foundation against sloping ground, of baseboard against clapboard, of round-headed storm window against rectangular trim, of black and green against creamy white, and of old bottles against lace curtains, quietly affirms the survival of Lunenburg's domestic building traditions in the present day.

RIGHT: 71 DUKE STREET – c1883

From underneath the massive "fan" brackets on the old James Kirby house, it is possible to see clear down to the Front Harbour, six blocks away. Similar views can be gained along all of the Old Town's north-south streets.

52 KAULBACK STREET – C1873

*Two houses on one town lot! This unusual, vertically-propor-
tioned structure, the Thomas Naas house, was built directly
behind the old Godfrey house about 1873. The old Godfrey
house was later used as a builder's workshop (by contractor
Hedley Pyke), then taken down and replaced with a new
house in 1920.*

58 TOWNSEND STREET — C1816

This house was purchased in 1816, partially finished, for use as a Rectory for St. John's Anglican Church. The Society for the Propogation of the Gospel put up some of the funds and the rest of the money was to come from the St. John's congregation, but they were divided over the wisdom of the purchase and could not come up with the cash. Instead, they put the Rector, the Rev. Robert Aitken and his successor, the Rev. James Cochran to work as carpenters to complete the house. The house is one of about nine buildings in the town that survive from the first two decades of the nineteenth century. The chimneys were removed about 1990.

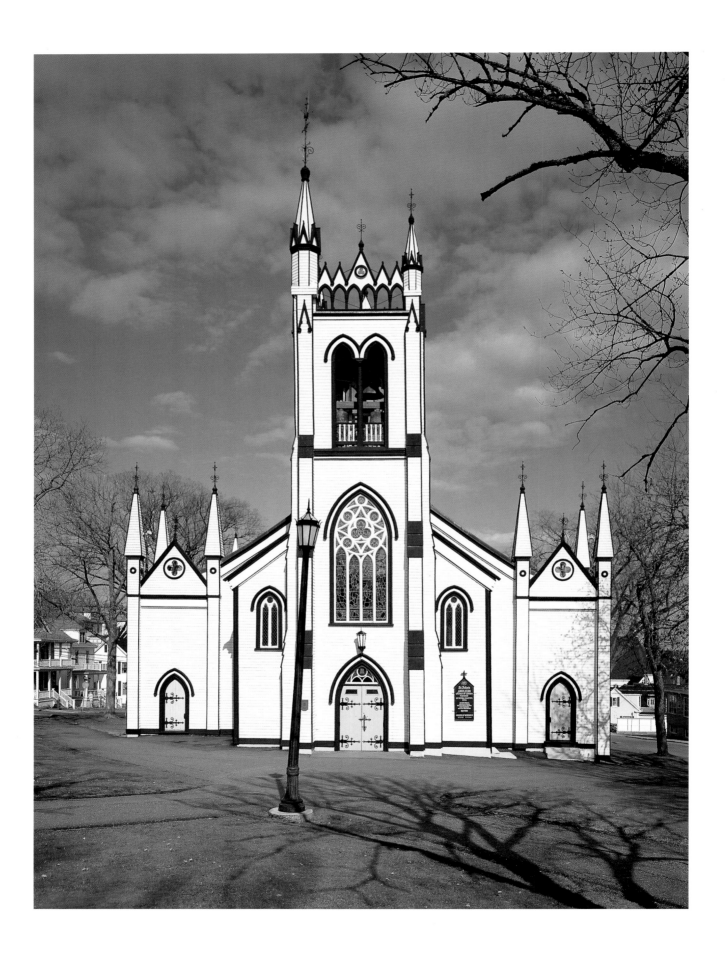

St. John's is the second oldest Anglican church in Canada (after St. Paul's in Halifax) and dates back to 1754, when the Lords of Trade and Plantations (the British colonial government administrators) granted £500 for its construction. The oak frame was brought to Lunenburg from Boston and may have come from the old Kings Chapel in that city. Originally built in the austere New England Meeting House style, the church was not completed until 1763, when the Society for the Propogation of the Gospel granted a further £250 to make it "neat and commodious." Until the 1770s, St. John's was Lunenburg's only church, and it was used by the Lutherans and Presbyterians as well as the Anglicans. It originally had an interior balcony on three sides, a 28 foot-high, plastered ceiling, and a small tower. In 1840, the original tower was replaced by a new tower, twelve feet square and seventy feet high with "handsome pinnacles in the Gothic style," designed by William Lawson, a member of the congregation. Between 1870 and 1875, when it was already well over one hundred years old, the church was completely reconditioned and "Gothicized" according to plans drawn by the Halifax architect David Stirling. The entire building was moved 25 feet to the west to enable the addition of a chancel at the eastern end; the tower was rebuilt (in the form that it is seen today); the nave was widened by ten feet; new lancet windows were installed; and the old plastered ceiling was removed–all at a cost of about $5,300. In 1892, a "committee of carpenters" headed by Solomon Morash designed further additions in the Gothic style–the side aisles were added on each side of the nave, more Gothic pinnacles were added all around the building, and massive hammer beams were installed on the interior. The church today is one of the most striking early wooden churches in the country and perhaps the very best example of the "Carpenter Gothic" style. It is particularly remarkable for the way that its form honestly reveals the alterations that have been made over its lifetime, and it sits like a serene jewel in the centre of the Old Town.

BELOW: REAR OF ST. JOHN'S ANGLICAN CHURCH

ST. ANDREW'S PRESBYTERIAN CHURCH – 1828

St. Andrews Church is notable on several counts, not the least of which is that it has a codfish for a weathervane. It also has the oldest Presbyterian congregation in Canada. Its first Calvinist communicants worshipped in the open air when Lunenburg was founded in 1753, under preacher Michael Ley, a Swiss blacksmith. They then used St. John's Anglican Church for about eleven years before building their own church in 1770, under the ministry of Rev. Bruin Romkes Comingo, whose fifty-year service (1770-1820) is commemorated to this day in a stone monument on the church grounds. The first church was replaced by the present structure in 1828. Designed by a Mr. Dechman, of Halifax, and constructed by a

Mr. Grant, a Scotsman, the new church was built for a cost of £1,200. In 1879, it was lengthened to 83 ft., widened to 40 ft., "Gothicized" with new lancet windows, and treated to a new spire. The church was further modified in 1909, when a new chancel was added to the eastern end. The six foot-long, codfish weathervane, constructed of beaten copper, was added in 1977 when repair work was carried out on the spire, and was chosen for its double symbolism–the cod as a symbol of Lunenburg's economy and the fish as an early Christian symbol. The old house next door (photo centre) was originally owned by the church and was rented during the 1850s to a Miss Gow, who ran a school in two downstairs rooms.

ST. NORBERT'S CATHOLIC CHURCH — c1840

The Catholic congregation in Lunenburg has always been small compared to other congregations, and this is reflected in the relatively small scale of St. Norbert's Church. Built about 1840, during the ministry of Rev. Edmond Doyle (who, according to the historian DesBrisay, travelled among his scattered parishioners with "a pair of small ponies"), the church is an interesting combination of British Neo-Classical/New England Meeting House form and Lunenburg Carpenter Gothic detail. Between 1890 and 1935, the congregation was not large enough to support the building, and it was closed for forty-five years. The spire was originally much taller than it is today, and was shortened to its present "witches hat" shape sometime after 1890. A large ell (photo left) was built in 1982 in the same style as the original structure, repeating the shapes of the original double lancet windows and simplified wooden buttresses.

WESTERN END OF FOX STREET

This streetscape, looking east along Fox Street from Kaulback, illustrates several generations of architectural change. The red house in the distance is the old Lennox tavern, dating from about 1804. The Zion Lutheran Church in the middle distance dates from 1891 and is the third church to have been built on the same site. The mansard-roofed house next to the church was built in the 1880s by Nicholas Berringer, a carpenter and wharf owner. Berringer also built the large Four-Square house in the foreground at about the same time, after moving an earlier house from that site over to the lot between the two houses. That old house was acquired twenty years later, about 1908, by Hedley Pyke, a contractor, who tore it down and replaced it with the small gable-roofed house seen in the photo. Missing from the photo are the old Lutheran manse, which stood next to the church until 1973, and a fourth storey tower, which once topped the Lunenburg Bump on the foreground Berringer house.

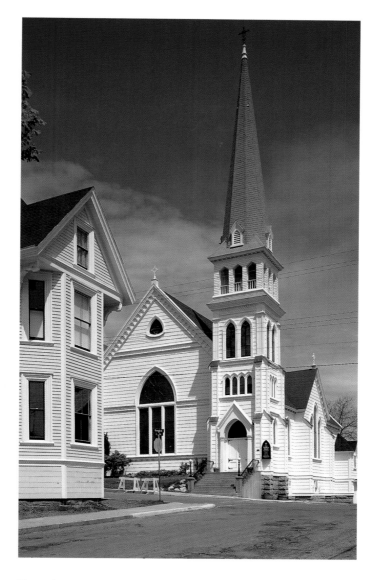

ZION LUTHERAN CHURCH — 1890/91

Zion Evangelical Lutheran Church has been described as the "Rock of Lutheranism" in Canada. It is home to the oldest worshipping Lutheran congregation in the country, which dates back to the earliest days of the Lunenburg settlement when the "foreign Protestants" held their services in the open air. The first Lutheran church was erected on this site in 1770, during the ministry of Rev. Frederick Schultz. The second was built in 1841, during the ministry of Rev. Carl Ernst Cossman. The present church was erected in 1891. It was designed in High Victorian Gothic style by Halifax architect Henry Busch, a Lutheran, and was built by George Boehner & Sons of West LaHave. The present church contains several artifacts and features that link it with the early history of the congregation. The "money chest," a four-foot by fifteen-inch, iron-lined, hardwood collection box brought from Germany with the first settlers, still exists. The Antoine-Marie bell, retrieved from the fall of Fortress Louisbourg in 1758 and purchased by the Lunenburg Lutherans in 1776, is kept in the church sanctuary. A large, stained glass window, set in the south wall of the church, is dedicated to Reverend Cossman who, during his forty-one-year ministry, travelled annually more than 4,000 miles on horseback around Lunenburg, Queens, and Halifax Counties, preaching in German. He was described in 1880 as "the living link which connects us today with the proud historic past." Reverend Cossman died in 1897 at age ninety-one and is buried in Hillcrest Cemetery, one block away from the church, along Fox Street.

69 TOWNSEND STREET – C1785

For many years the residence of Judge George T. Solomon, this house was built by Henry Koch, a "gentleman and sawmiller," using "coulisse" construction. It was Victorianized in the 1880s with the addition of a three-storey, Lunenburg Bump. This was taken off in 1974 and the house was restored to its original Georgian style. Zion Lutheran Church can be seen in the background.

69 FOX STREET – C1804

Restored in 1994 to its former glory, the Lennox Tavern was one of Lunenburg's early watering holes. Ironically, by 1879 it was in use as a "Temperance House" and is identified as such on the 1879 Bird's Eye View of the town. In the present day, the old tavern is a registered Provincial Heritage Property in a residential district where drinking establishments are proscribed by modern zoning regulations.

89 York Street — c1828

Known as the "Blair House" from the name of its mid 19th-century owner, John Blair, a shoemaker and leatherworker, this is a transitional house that combines the central chimney typical of 18th-century Cape Cod houses with the five-bay facade typical of later Georgian houses. It was damaged by fire in the 1960s and restored by new owners in the 1970s.

59 DUKE STREET – c1833

This house is intimately connected with the Lunenburg fishery through two long-term family ownerships. It was built in 1833 by William Ross, who was a West India merchant with wharf and warehouse premises down on the waterfront. It was owned by his heirs until 1910, when it passed to Angus Beck, a teamster with W.C. Smith & Co. (the precursor of today's National Sea Products), by whose family it was owned until 1965. Both owners could walk to work along Duke Street, a short five blocks downhill to the harbour.

71 DUKE STREET — C1888

*Pointed dormers were the hallmark of the Gothic Revival style.
James Kirby, owner of the James Kirby Furniture Depot, gave
the style a distinctly Lunenburg look when he built this giant
house and added a projecting, rectangular bay under the
dormer. The huge attic area was once used as a gymnasium
and training space by Billie King, who achieved local fame as
an acrobat and juggler.*

201 York Street — c1893

In an eclectic combination of Gothic and Second Empire styling, the Robert Herman House sits at the "back of town" on York Street, near the top of Blockhouse Hill.

58 HOPSON STREET – C1883

*Bernard and Napier Smith, two fishermen, built this house
about 1883. They chose the popular Lunenburg Bump style,
but gave it a two-tiered, bell-cast roof. They also decided to
place two recessed "rolling pin" panels over the door, and a
line of scroll-sawn running trim under the five-sided dormer.*

43 YORK STREET — C1881

Allan R. Morash went further than anyone else in the town in his interpretation of the Lunenburg Bump style. His baroque architectural concoction of quasi-Oriental, Italianate influences reflects the many facets of his own life. He was a working partner in the waterfront firm of Lewis Anderson & Co., member of the first Town Council, Mayor of Lunenburg from 1902-1909, and, later, a Member of Parliament. He

directed the Lunenburg Brass Band and taught music from a studio built, in an equally fanciful but thoroughly different style, on the back of the house. He was a violinist, and the story is told that, after his death, he could be heard playing along with his wife, Clara, a pianist, who outlived him by thirteen years. The house was built by his cousins, John and Joseph Morash and his father, Charles Morash.

LUNENBURG ACADEMY (REAR VIEW)

*The Academy is Lunenburg's most prominent landmark.
Situated on top of Gallows Hill at the western edge of the Old
Town, it is visible from miles away and is still referred to by
many people as "the castle on the hill." All Lunenburg children
go to this school (it originally served all grades but is now
used for elementary only) and it is probably the only building
in town that absolutely every resident has been inside at some
point in their life. It was built in 1894/95 as a replacement for
an earlier Academy that stood in the Parade Square, near the
Town Hall, but which burned down in 1893. After the fire,
there was a controversial public debate over whether the new
school should be built on Blockhouse Hill or Gallows Hill. The*

*latter site won the day with Mayor S. Watson Oxner casting
the deciding vote. The architect was Harry H. Mott, originally
from Saint John, N.B., but working at that time out of Halifax.
The building contract was secured by the Oxford Furniture
Company at an agreed price of $25,000 and construction
began in the autumn of 1894. The builders went bankrupt
halfway through the contract, however, and the work was
continued under the direction of local master-builders Joseph
and Solomon Morash. The final cost was about $30,000 and
the Academy was opened on November 7, 1895. Each floor is
laid out with six entrances, six classrooms, and six staircases
up to the next floor. The interior is finished in birch and ash.*

The basement is a labyrinth of boiler rooms and utility rooms. There is an assembly hall on the third floor, and a 600lb bell in the front tower. There were originally four towers, but the one on the north-east was removed in the early 1960s after it became rotten.The third floor was closed in the late 1960s, when a new Junior/Senior High School was built, but has recently been partially re-opened as part of a restoration plan undertaken by the Lunenburg Academy Foundation.

NEW TOWN
AND THE TANYARD

HISTORIC LUNENBURG extended beyond Old Town, as defined by the British model plan of 1753. In the areas surrounding the original town lots, surveyors laid out common lands, garden lots, and farm lots during the earliest years. Sawmills and gristmills were also established, and land was granted for the purposes of a tanyard on the opposite shore of Front Harbour. Thus, present-day Tannery Road runs through one of the oldest areas of settlement.

As Lunenburg developed in its second century, the town entered an era of increasing prosperity, and its population began to exceed the confines of Old Town. In 1862, regions of the common land immediately west and east of Old Town were subdivided into building lots. A large eighty-lot subdivision was established to the northwest of Front Harbour. Increased by nearly one-half its area in 1878, this district became known as New Town. It constituted the principal area of expansion in Lunenburg in the nineteenth century.

The lower streets of Old Town connect with New Town by funnelling into a westward extension of Lincoln Street, which joins with New Town's Dufferin and Falkland streets at a common intersection. Walking down Falkland, past the complex of early twentieth-century structures that comprise Lunenburg Foundry & Engineering's main plant, one can turn onto Tannery Road and enjoy a short, level hike to the entrance of the Lunenburg Golf Club. Along the way, there are superb, uninterrupted views across the harbour of the waterfront, of Old Town, and of the harbour entrance.

New Town is well worth exploring. A number of elaborate houses were built here during the heyday of the West Indies trade and the Grand Banks fishery. New Town's somewhat larger building lots provide, in several instances, a more gracious setting for Lunenburg's spirited expressions of the various Victorian architectural revivals.

In this photo, the random chimneys and added-as-needed industrial buildings of the Lunenburg Foundry, on the edge of the New Town, contrast with the carefully placed towers and formal, Second Empire design of the Lunenburg Academy, in the distance on the edge of the Old Town. Each building represents a different but equally balanced side of Lunenburg's character as a town. The Academy, on the one hand, represents form, classicism, concern for outward appearance, and pride in architecture. The Foundry, on the other, represents adaptiveness, improvisation,

practicality and the priority of function over form. The Foundry was incorporated in 1907, when a group of Lunenburg businessmen, under the leadership of John J. Kinley, rebuilt the fire-damaged plant of the old Lunenburg Iron Company. The first cast was made in July, 1908 and the plant has been in continuous operation ever since. The company at first produced stoves and related iron products but later moved into production of marine engines and equipment such as steering gear, windlasses, hoists, etc. In 1921 it undertook the first refit of a Lunenburg schooner with a diesel engine and, from then on, was in the forefront of the design, manufacture, and installation of marine gear for the fishing industry. During the Second World War, the Foundry refitted 104 ships for the Canadian Navy, converted 8 whaling ships to minesweepers for the Norwegian Navy, and refitted 70 tugs and two RCAF supply ships. Today, it continues as one of the town's largest marine service employers and still produces woodstoves.

ABOVE LEFT: *The tradition of change in Lunenburg's architecture continues through to the present day. In this photo, the triangular eaves return on the left (just above the rhododendron) belongs to the Henry Adams House, built in the New Town in the 1860s. The pedimented dormer and balcony railing in the centre of the photo, and the rear ell of which they are a part, were added in 1902. The tower in the background was added to the house next door in the late 1980s.*

ABOVE RIGHT: *The Old Town is connected to the New Town by the westward extension of Lincoln Street. In this view, two towers are all that remain of four that once overlooked the street. The tower in the foreground was built by Edwin Naas about 1891. The one in the background was built about 1888 on a building that is still known as the place where Joey Boliver had his grocery store.*

75 Dufferin Street — c1875/1895

In 1893, C. Edwin Kaulback, barrister, ship-owner, and M.P. for Lunenburg County, bought the old Edward Rafuse house for $10 at a sheriff's sale and began its transformation into "Mitzpah Cottage." Whether he had the work done all at once or piece-by-piece (as each ship came in) is unknown, but the result today is a highly interesting architectural amalgam of bay windows, ornamental brackets, decorative shingle patterns, beaded vergeboards, multiple entrances, and gabled roofs, all capped by a hip-roofed cupola (which, in this photo, peeks over the rooftop). The "cottage" was only a half mile from Mr. Kaulback's main residence in the Old Town. Even today, many Lunenburgers maintain cottages close to town.

48 DUFFERIN STREET – 1889

This fanciful house was built by Captain Albert King. It was purchased three years later by Burgess McIttrick, the first principal of the Lunenburg Academy, who lived in it with his wife, Mary, for fifty years. It was later the home of Joey Boliver,

who ran a grocery store at the foot of Dufferin Hill (or "Apple Tree Hill" as it is sometimes still called). The tower roof and its four lookout windows were reconstructed in 1994.

26 DUFFERIN STREET – C1890

Sitting at the foot of Dufferin Street, next to where the railway tracks used to be (the roof of the train station can be seen in the bottom right of the photo), this house was built by Reuben Conrad, the town's first Superintendent of Streets. From 1924 onwards it was operated as the "Hillside Hotel." Recently restored as the "Lunenburg Inn," the form of the house and its tower are tastefully defined by a new red roof and a complimentary paint scheme.

10 FALKLAND STREET — c1886

The Bluenose Lodge was built by Charles Morash, a prosperous house builder, in a combination of French Second Empire and High Victorian Gothic style. Situated at the intersection of the roads to Bridgewater and Mahone Bay, it is one of the most prominent buildings in the New Town. Captain Karl Kohler lived in the house for twenty years from 1921 to 1946, when it was purchased by Claude Vincent and turned into a lodge. The single storey dining room was added at that time.

6 LORNE STREET – C1867

Known as "Rose Cottage," this house was built in 1867 by carpenter James Kirby for Thomas Curll, a businessman and land developer. After several changes of ownership, it was acquired in 1889 by James Hirtle, a prominent clothing merchant, member of the first Town Council, and owner of the

"Hirtle Block" (where Tim Hortons Coffee Shop is now located). The house originally had a simple, peaked Gothic dormer on the front but, by 1896, it had been transformed into the octagonal turret that can be seen today.

18 FALKLAND STREET — C1862

James D. Eisenhauer was owner of a waterfront outfitting business, a major shareholder in the Nova Scotia Central Railway (connecting Lunenburg with Middleton, Nova Scotia), MLA for Lunenburg in the 1860s and 1870s, and MP for Lunenburg County in 1887. He purchased this "Fisherman's Gothic" house in 1870 from fancy goods merchant Joseph Lockhart, for a price of $1,700. The house was one of the first to be built when the New Town lots first became available in 1862. Falkland Street at that time had an uninterrupted view of the harbour and was a fashionable location for the town's wealthy and successful citizens to reside. James Eisenhauer's house was the first in the town to have electric lights.

26 FALKLAND STREET — C1862

This house, originally known as "Floral Cottage," was built in 1862 for Charles Hewitt, a sailmaker and partner in the firm of Hewitt & Adams. It originally had a simple Gothic dormer over the front door. The well-proportioned Lunenburg Bump was added in the 1880s. The rear tower, which is connected to a mansard roofed wing, was added by 1893. The open porch on the left side of the house was added in the 1930s. Charles was a member of the first Town Council. His daughter, Minnie Hewitt, a teacher and first vice-principal of the Lunenburg Academy, lived in the house until her death in 1963.

21 FALKLAND STREET — c1887

Shipbuilder John B. Young built this house after both the house in which he had been living and his nearby shipyard were displaced by the extension of the railway along the Lunenburg waterfront. The Town Council minutes record a protracted debate over the width of the railway right-of-way and the proposed location of the station, but do not record what settlement John Young received. Presumably, it was sufficient to finance the construction of his new house. The trees along Falkland Street were planted at about the same time.

REAR 17 YOUNG STREET — 1880S

The Lunenburg Bump serves several functions. On the ground level, it functions as a storm porch. On the upper level, it brings light and space to the upstairs hall and enables residents to get a good, elevated view out of the house, whether along the street or, as in this case, out to the harbour. With the inclusion of a door, it can also function as a fire escape. Here, the Bump on the back of the old John Young/Joseph Young house is a study in function, form, and well-placed detail.

38 FALKLAND STREET — C1866

On many Lunenburg Bumps, the dormer extends out further than the lower storm porch. On a few, as in this photo, the porch is the more protruding feature. Here, the five-sided dormer is connected to the rectangular porch by an interesting, curved intermediate roof, which allows the bracketted cornice of the porch to take visual prominence. This Bump is also unusual in that its entrance is on the side. Wooden storm windows affirm the complete intactness of this house, which was built for Henry Adams, a sailmaker and partner in Hewitt & Adams.

52 Tannery Road — c1825

Shortly after Lunenburg was founded, land on the south side of the Front harbour was granted for the purpose of establishing tanneries on several small brooks that flowed to the shore. The area became known, and is still known, as "the Tanyard." This Cape Cod house is the oldest building in the area and was probably built by Christian Rhuland, who bought the old tannery buildings in 1825. He later sold to Jacob Sperry who sold, in turn, to Jasper Burns, in whose family the house and tannery remained for three generations, until 1946. Although now vinyl-sided on the front facade, the house still retains the simple grace of the early Cape Cod style, with a central chimney, low eaves, three-quarter Cape design, and a wooden storm door.

42 FALKLAND — C1887

William N. Zwicker was a senior member of Zwicker & Company, the oldest fishing company in Lunenburg, as well as a dry and fancy goods merchant. He purchased this house from another merchant, George Geldert, in 1890 for $5,000.00. The eclectic, High Victorian Gothic-Italianate-

Bracketted style of the building is rare in Lunenburg, and the house has some of the last surviving Victorian "gingerbread" bargeboards in the town. The house was restored in the late 1980s and the roof turret (not an original feature) was added at that time.

AFTERWORD

IN DECEMBER 1995, the United Nations Educational, Social, and Cultural Organization (UNESCO) World Heritage Committee added Lunenburg's Old Town to the World Heritage List—a list of cultural sites of outstanding universal value worthy of designation and protection under the 1972 World Heritage Convention.

World Heritage Listing is, first and foremost, an honour and a confirmation of Lunenburg's deep historic significance. The Old Town is one of the best surviving examples of eighteenth-century British colonial town planning in North America. It is one of the most distinctive and architecturally cohesive historic towns anywhere in Canada. And it is a place where historical themes run deep through traditional industries, long-established religious affiliations, linguistic characteristics, and cultural traits. World Heritage Listing is a recognition that these particularities of urban form, architecture, history, and culture make Lunenburg a community like no other in the world.

It is also a recognition that Lunenburg's architectural heritage is vulnerable and in need of protection. While the town has remained remarkably intact, with about 80 per cent of old buildings retaining their original character, it has not been immune to demolition, inappropriate alteration, and unsympathetic new construction. World Heritage Listing does not, in itself, provide statutory protection. Instead, it places responsibility for conservation at the local level—with property owners to ensure that their buildings are well maintained and with the Town Council to ensure that adequate protective mechanisms are in place. Fortunately, most property owners live up to this responsibility and the Council has adopted protective regulations under the provincial Planning Act and Heritage Property Act.

What does World Heritage status mean for the future of Lunenburg? It will almost certainly bring a significant increase in tourism and a demand for more tourist facilities. It will undoubtedly lead to the conversion of more houses and buildings into bed and breakfasts, hotels, restaurants, gift shops, and entertainment facilities. It may lead to pressure for a greater proportion of the waterfront to be given over to tourism, and difficult questions of tourism development versus traditional marine industrial use will then have to be addressed. It may also mean that the town will have to be wary of commercialization and loss of authenticity, whether it be through garish signs, overindulgence in stereotypical images of the "quaint" Bluenose fisherman, or shallow, "theme park" representations of the town's history.

On the other hand, it may be that World Heritage status will encourage such a renaissance of interest in authentic restoration and quality rehabilitation that fears of unsympathetic development will prove unfounded, and conservation regulations will gather dust in the Town Hall. With the World Heritage significance of the town officially recognized, it is also possible that new sources of public funding for conservation may become available, whether from within Canada or from UNESCO, thus further encouraging development to be carried out in a manner respectful of the designation.

It is certain, though, that World Heritage Listing will bring economic benefit along with a renewed awareness of the cultural value of the town and the many levels on which it can be appreciated.

208/210 MONTAGUE STREET c1827

A double house with Scottish dormers and Italianate storm porches. Built for Captain Jacob Moser. One side is maintained in its original style, the other is vinyl-sided.

NEW TOWN

THE TANYARD